Heroes for Young Readers

Written by Renee Taft Meloche
Illustrated by Bryan Pollard

Gladys Aylward
Corrie ten Boom
William Carey
Amy Carmichael
Jim Elliot
Jonathan Goforth
Betty Greene
Adoniram Judson
Eric Liddell
David Livingstone
Lottie Moon
George Müller
Nate Saint
Mary Slessor
Hudson Taylor
Cameron Townsend

…and more coming soon.

Heroes for Young Readers are based on the *Christian Heroes: Then & Now*
biographies by Janet and Geoff Benge. Don't miss out on these exciting,
true adventures for ages ten and up! See the back of this book for a full
listing of the biographies loved by children, parents, and teachers.

For a free catalog of books and materials contact
YWAM Publishing, P.O. Box 55787, Seattle, WA 98155
1-800-922-2143, www.ywampublishing.com

HEROES FOR YOUNG READERS

WILLIAM CAREY

Bearer of Good News

Written by Renee Taft Meloche
Illustrated by Bryan Pollard

PUBLISHING
P.O. BOX 55787 / SEATTLE, WA 98155

William Carey: Bearer of Good News · Text copyright © 2002 by Renee Taft Meloche · Illustrations © 2002 by Bryan Pollard
Published by YWAM Publishing, P.O. Box 55787, Seattle, WA 98155   ISBN 1-57658-236-1   Printed in China.   All rights reserved.

A preacher, William Carey, sailed
        in seventeen ninety-three
from England's shore to India
        with great expectancy.

He took a boat and traveled up
        a river, where he spied
amazing new and wondrous sights
        along the riverside.

The Indian women balanced baskets
        on their heads and wore
bright dresses they called saris, while
        the men along the shore
had turbans wrapped around their heads
        and wore wide floppy pants.
As William took in all he saw,
        he gladly gave God thanks.

For this was an adventure he
        had dreamed about for years,
although most Christians at that time
        would never volunteer
to go to far-off places where
        the Bible was not known.
Most Christians felt more comfortable
        with staying right at home.

But William felt that Christians should
go out and share God's word
in places all around the world
with those who'd never heard.

The boat stopped at a village and
         he got out to explore
the marketplace, where he saw things
         he'd never seen before.

The merchants sold dried fish and sandals,
         brass, and silverware,
as unfamiliar scents and noises
         filled the open air.

As William looked around, he knew
         that most had never heard
about the Christian God or ever
         read His Holy Word.

So first he had to learn the language
         spoken all around:
Bengali was the language in
         the country and in town.

And, fortunately, William had
         a love and fascination
for languages, though he'd not had
         much formal education.

He'd studied language on his own
         and worked wholeheartedly
till he spoke Latin, Greek, and Hebrew
         with great fluency.

It wasn't long until he'd learned
     Bengali and he knew
that he could start to do the work
     that he'd set out to do.

He wanted to translate God's Word
     into the Indian tongue.
His knowledge of their language now
     would help to get that done.

The months passed by and then one night
     some Hindus—quite devout—
came with a goat to William's house
     and asked him to come out.

"Please come and sacrifice this goat
     to Kali," said one man.
"We must please her or she might punish
     us and harm our land."

Now William knew that Hindus had
    a lot of gods of stone
who must be kept quite happy and,
    if not, what Hindus owned
would be destroyed—their homes and crops
    and even families.
This may sound strange to Christians, but
    it's what Hindus believed.

So William said, "I serve a God
    who lives and loves all life.
My God forgives, and He expects
    no living sacrifice."

He told the Hindus more about
    the God we serve today;
but fearful of their gods, they killed
    the poor goat anyway.

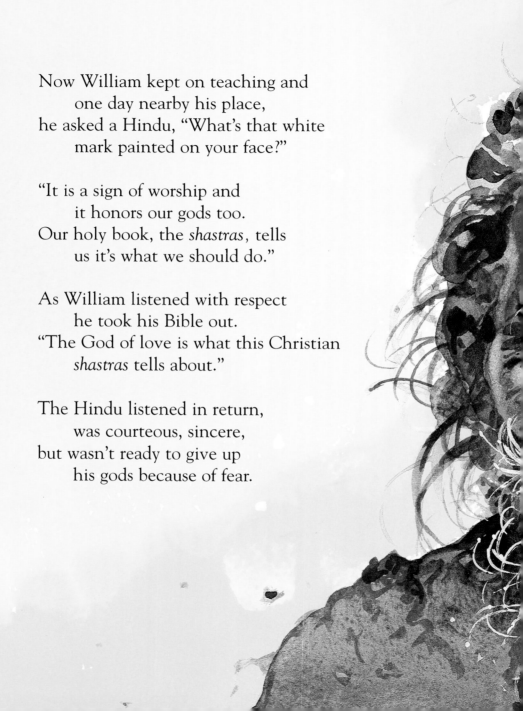

Now William kept on teaching and
    one day nearby his place,
he asked a Hindu, "What's that white
    mark painted on your face?"

"It is a sign of worship and
    it honors our gods too.
Our holy book, the *shastras*, tells
    us it's what we should do."

As William listened with respect
    he took his Bible out.
"The God of love is what this Christian
    shastras tells about."

The Hindu listened in return,
    was courteous, sincere,
but wasn't ready to give up
    his gods because of fear.

Four years passed by, and hundreds came
      whenever William preached,
yet not a single Hindu was
      converted by his speech.

He hoped the first translation of
      the gospels—when complete—
would help him be persuasive with
      new Hindus he would meet.

He bought supplies, a printing press,
and fixed up a small room.
He printed many gospels of
the Bible and then, soon,
he hired some Indian helpers so
that many thousand sheets
of Scripture could be rolled and printed
every single week.

One day a Hindu, Krishna Pal,
    came to his house to hear
some stories of the Christian God.
    Weeks later he appeared
announcing he'd decided to
    become a Christian too.
He ate a meal at William's home,
    which Hindus could not do.

Soon others heard he'd eaten with
a Christian he'd befriended.
These Indians became angry and
in no time had descended
upon his home and waited in
the street till he appeared.
As Krishna Pal was rushing home,
they threw sharp rocks and jeered.

Although his wife and daughters all
        felt overcome by fear,
they soon became new Christians just
        as Christmastime grew near.

Then on December twenty-eighth,
        together they agreed
to all be baptized in a river
        as a family.

But when they saw the crowds of Hindus
        by the riverside
the family, except Krishna Pal,
        all grew so terrified
they changed their minds, yet William thought
        that he should still begin.
He spoke first in Bengali—
        and then he led a hymn.

Now Christians also had come out
to see this great event.
When Krishna Pal was baptized, they
all cheered encouragement.

More Hindus became Christians as
     the weeks and months passed by,
and copies of the Bible were
     passed out in great supply.

Now William spent time studying
     and learning all he could
about the Sanskrit language that
     the wealthy understood.

When rich young Englishmen arrived
     and had to understand
the customs and the language of
     the people in the land,
it was quite clear that William's skills
     would soon be in demand.
So he became a college teacher—
     something he'd not planned.

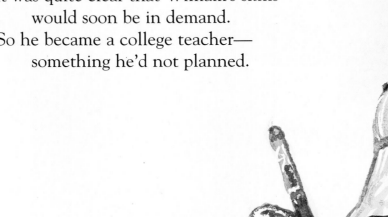

And William really loved the job
of teaching Indian ways.
He had more reason to rejoice
when in the coming days
the daughters and the wife of
Krishna Pal all came to find
the courage to be baptized and
to leave their fears behind.

Then one spring night in eighteen twelve
    the whole print shop burned down.
What William saw, with near despair,
    as he first looked around
was one big pile of twisted, melted
    iron and charred wood.
So many years of his hard work
    had now been lost for good.

His multilanguage dictionary
    that was finally done,
new versions of the Bible, and
    translations he'd begun—
they all were lost, and William wept
    because so much was gone.
He had a choice to make: should he
    give up or still go on?

He chose to put his trust in God
and knew God would be near.
If William kept his faith and patience
he could persevere.

To help replace the ruined shop,
donations soon poured in,
and in a few short months the press
was printing once again.

Years later, William Carey died,
   in eighteen thirty-four.
He left the world a better place
   than it had been before.

Translations of the Bible had
   been printed and then spread
throughout the land of India
   and are, today, well read.

Still many speak in languages
   that are to us unknown
without a written alphabet
   or Bible of their own.

They need someone, like William, to
    have God's own Word translated,
so His forgiveness and great love
    can be communicated.

Christian Heroes: Then & Now

by Janet and Geoff Benge

√Gladys Aylward: The Adventure of a Lifetime
Rowland Bingham: Into Africa's Interior
. ord Corrie ten Boom: Keeper of the Angels' Den
William Booth: Soup, Soap, and Salvation
William Carey: Obliged to Go
√Amy Carmichael: Rescuer of Precious Gems
Loren Cunningham: Into All the World
Jim Elliot: One Great Purpose
Jonathan Goforth: An Open Door in China
Betty Greene: Wings to Serve
Wilfred Grenfell: Fisher of Men
Adoniram Judson: Bound for Burma
√Eric Liddell: Something Greater Than Gold
David Livingstone: Africa's Trailblazer
Lottie Moon: Giving Her All for China
George Müller: The Guardian of Bristol's Orphans
Nate Saint: On a Wing and a Prayer
Ida Scudder: Healing Bodies, Touching Hearts
Sundar Singh: Footprints over the Mountains
Mary Slessor: Forward into Calabar
Hudson Taylor: Deep in the Heart of China
Cameron Townsend: Good News in Every Language
Lillian Trasher: The Greatest Wonder in Egypt
John Williams: Messenger of Peace
Florence Young: Mission Accomplished

Heroes of History

by Janet and Geoff Benge

John Adams: Independence Forever
Clara Barton: Courage under Fire
Daniel Boone: Frontiersman
George Washington Carver: From Slave to Scientist
Meriwether Lewis: Off the Edge of the Map
Abraham Lincoln: A New Birth of Freedom
Douglas MacArthur: What Greater Honor
William Penn: Liberty and Justice for All
Theodore Roosevelt: An American Original
Harriet Tubman: Freedombound
George Washington: True Patriot

...and more coming soon. Unit study curriculum guides are also available.

For a free catalog of books and materials contact
YWAM Publishing, P.O. Box 55787, Seattle, WA 98155
1-800-922-2143, www.ywampublishing.com

B
Car   Meloche, Renee Taft
        William Carey

DATE DUE			
NOV 17 06			
NOV 16 07			
SEP 21 10			
MAR 29 11			